ON THE JOB

Creative Careers

Be a VIDEO GAME DESIGNER!

Theresa Emminizer

PowerKiDS press

Published in 2025 by The Rosen Publishing Group, Inc.
2544 Clinton Street, Buffalo, NY 14224

First Edition

Editor: Theresa Emminizer
Book Design: Michael Flynn

Photo Credits: aslysun/Shutterstock.com; (series background) KanokpolTokumhnerd/Shutterstock.com; (series boxes) vector illustration/Shutterstock.com; p. 4 BONDART PHOTOGRAPHY/Shutterstock.com; p. 5 Monkey Business Images/Shutterstock.com; p. 7 New Africa/Shutterstock.com; p. 9 Frame Stock Footage/Shutterstock.com; p. 11 DC Studio/Shutterstock.com; p. 13 Evgeny Atamanenko/Shutterstock.com; p. 15 Ganna Tokolova/Shutterstock.com; p. 17 Gorodenkoff/Shutterstock.com; p. 19 PeopleImages.com - Yuri A/Shutterstock.com; p. 21 SofikoS/Shutterstock.com; p. 22 Rovsky/Shutterstock.com; p. 23 DC Studio/Shutterstock.com; p. 25 Gorodenkoff/Shutterstock.com; p. 27 Sergey Novikov/Shutterstock.com; p. 29 Viacheslav Lopatin/Shutterstock.com.

Cataloging-in-Publication Data

Names: Emminizer, Theresa.
Title: Be a videogame designer! / Theresa Emminizer.
Description: Buffalo, NY : PowerKids Press, 2025. | Series: On the job: creative careers | Includes glossary and index.
Identifiers: ISBN 9781499449570 (pbk.) | ISBN 9781499449587 (library bound) | ISBN 9781499449594 (ebook)
Subjects: LCSH: Video games–Design–Vocational guidance–Juvenile literature. | Video games industry–Vocational guidance–Juvenile literature. | Video games–Programming–Vocational guidance–Juvenile literature.
Classification: LCC GV1469.3 E49 2025 | DDC 794.8'1536–dc23

Manufactured in the United States of America

Some of the images in this book illustrate individuals who are models. The depictions do not imply actual situations or events.

CPSIA Compliance Information: Batch #CWPK25. For Further Information contact Rosen Publishing at 1-800-237-9932.

CONTENTS

A PASSION FOR PLAY

Do you love playing video games? Do you enjoy losing yourself in another world? Do you find yourself imagining new places, people, and things that could happen? If so, video game design might be the career path for you!

Video game designers create video games. They come up with an overall concept, or idea, of a game, how it will be played, and what a player's experience will be like. Video game design is both fun and challenging. Designers need to think outside the box to come up with ideas that stand out. They need to be good storytellers. They also need knowledge and special skills.

Do you have what it takes to be a video game designer?

DESIGNERS AND DEVELOPERS

What exactly does a video game designer do? They create the structure, rules, and gameplay of a video game! They create the plot, characters, and how a game plays out. Simply put, they are the masterminds behind video games. They create **virtual** worlds.

A video game designer is different from a game developer. Developers do the **technical** work of game creation. They're responsible for coding and programming. Game designers work closely with game developers to bring their ideas to life. Often, this involves a lot of trial and error to find out what works best.

LEARNING ON THE JOB!

Game designers sometimes draw storyboards to help communicate, or share, their ideas with teammates. Communication is a key part of creating a successful video game.

A storyboard is a series of pictures that show how a game should be **animated**.

MAKING A GAME

There are many steps involved in creating a video game. The first phase, or step, is conceptualization. Conceptualization is when the game designer comes up with the overall concept, or idea, of a game.

Next, the designer or design team must create a Game Design Document (GDD). This is a complete outline of the game and everything involved in it, such as the plot and mechanics, or working parts. This includes how a player moves through levels, how **interactive** features work within the game world, the pace of gameplay, and more. The GDD serves as a blueprint for the development team.

A GDD must be very well-thought-out so that the development team can follow the designer's ideas properly.

Working off the GDD, the designing and programming phase begins. The design team crafts character models and artwork for the game. The developer team begins coding and programming it. At this point, music may be composed, or written, for the game and actors may be hired to do speaking parts.

Next, a prototype is made and tested. A prototype is the first model of a game. This is tested by gamers, who give feedback about how the game works. The design and development team fix any problems that come up. The last stage of production is marketing. This is when the game is advertised and sold.

LEARNING ON THE JOB!

The time it takes to create a video game differs greatly based on the budget, or amount of money available, and size of the team involved. Some video games take years to complete.

Playtesting is having a group of users play unfinished versions of a game.

TYPES OF DESIGNERS

There are several different types of video game designers. They each work on different aspects, or parts, of the game.

- Gameplay designers focus on the basic workings of the game, its rules, and how players interact with things within it.
- Game level designers create the stages of play within the game. They map out the course of the game and decide how a player moves within it. They make sure the game isn't too slow or too hard.
- Game narrative designers create the game's storylines and script.
- Game UI (user interface) and UX (user experience) designers make sure a game is understandable and appealing to users.

Have you ever lost yourself in a video game? A video game designer, or team of designers, worked hard to create that world and experience for you!

LEARNING ON THE JOB!

In a small game **studio**, one video game designer might be responsible for all of the roles listed on page 12. Larger studios have bigger teams and more specialized roles.

EDUCATION

If you want to land a job in video game design, it's helpful to have a bachelor's degree from a college or university. A bachelor's degree usually takes four years to complete. Someone who wants to be a video game designer should study game design, computer animation, computer science, or another related field.

A good game design program will include the principles, or main ideas, of design and help students build the technical skills they'll need to do their work. This could include classes in computer programming, animation, **three-dimensional (3-D)** design, and digital media.

LEARNING ON THE JOB!

Attending an in-person college isn't the only way to learn the art of video game design. E-learning websites such as edX and Coursera also offer online game development courses so that students can learn from home.

Today, the University of Southern California has one of the top video game design programs in the country.

INTERNSHIPS

An internship is a temporary, or short-term, work experience in which a student or beginner can learn about an **industry** from a **professional**. Most major game studios such as Epic Games and Riot Games offer internships.

Internships are a great way to build hands-on experience. Interns get to see how a real design team works. Although interns don't usually lead projects, they get to contribute, or add to, them. Internships also help beginners build a network, or web of connections with other key players in the industry. Becoming an intern at a design studio could help you get a full-time job there later.

Landing an internship at a successful video game studio can make a big difference to your career.

BUILDING A PORTFOLIO

A portfolio is a collection of a video game designer's best work. Most video game designers have their own websites or online portfolios. This portfolio should include links to the games video game designers have made and other important projects they've worked on. It should be updated often. A portfolio is meant to show a designer's range of abilities and skills.

It's important for a portfolio to be eye-catching, easy to read, and memorable, or easy to remember. To compete with other designers, one needs to make their work stand out. Some designers tweak, or make small changes to, their portfolio when applying for a particular job or position.

LEARNING ON THE JOB!

A portfolio should include a way for recruiters, or people who look for people to hire for a job, to see and understand a game designer's process of brainstorming a game.

A portfolio is a way to show schools, jobs, and **clients** who a designer is.

WORK ENVIRONMENTS

What kind of environment, or place, can a video game designer expect to work in? Most game designers work in offices. They may work in large game development studios or entertainment companies.

Some video game designers work freelance. That means they're hired on a project-by-project basis. They sign a contract, or agreement, to do a certain amount of work for a client or company. Freelance designers may work from home.

No matter where a designer works, they're sure to spend a lot of time in front of a computer! They may also spend time in meetings with coworkers and clients.

Game designers often work with a team of other designers and developers.

SPECIAL SKILLS

In addition to education and hands-on experience, video game designers need special skills to do their job well. Designers need to be able to meet deadlines for projects. That means having good time management skills. They need to communicate clearly with teammates. They need to have patience and be able to problem-solve, especially when testing prototypes.

Above all, video game designers must be creative. They must imagine worlds, characters, and stories that feel real to players. These worlds must be fun, exciting, and just challenging enough to make people want to keep playing.

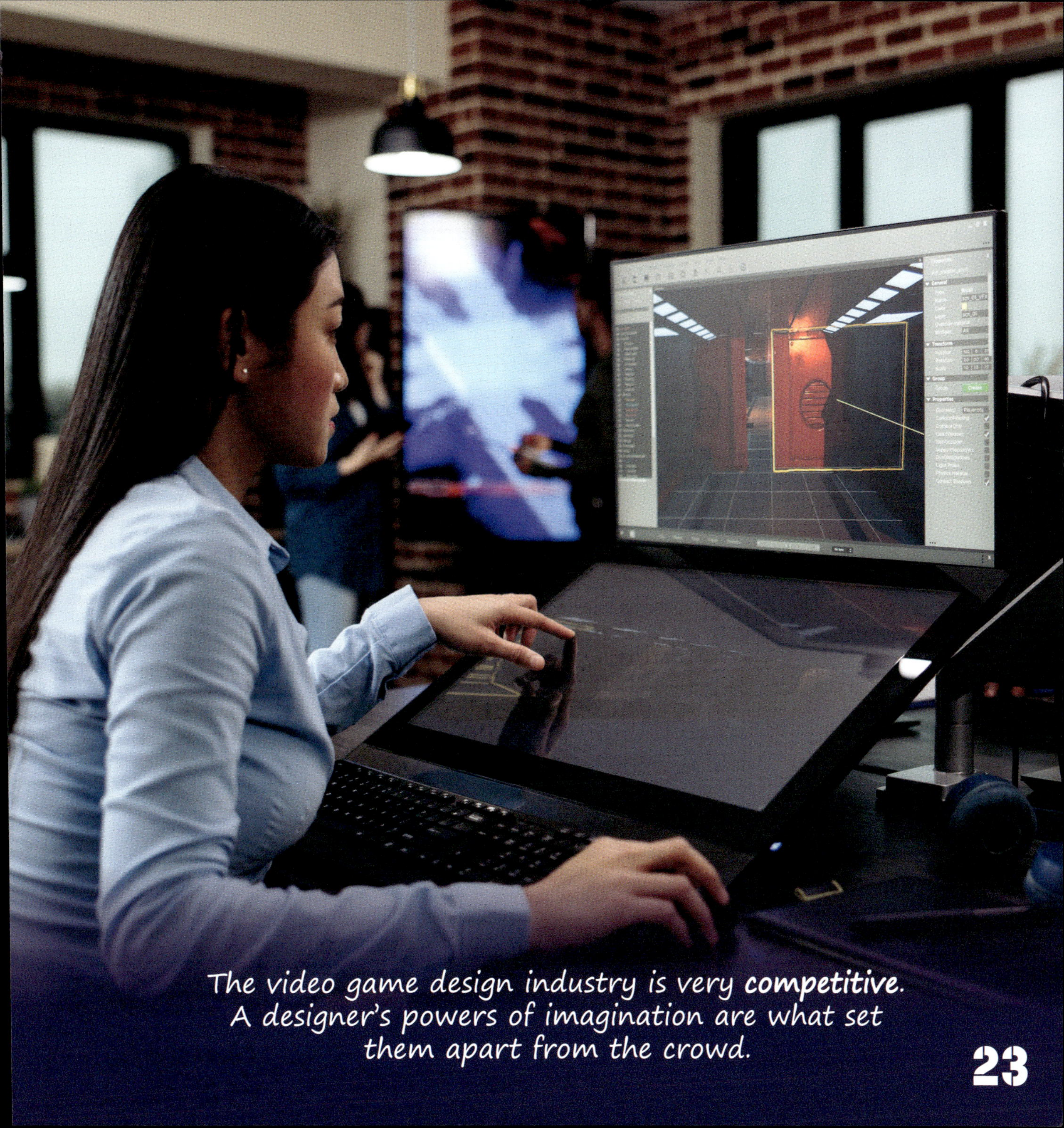

The video game design industry is very **competitive**. A designer's powers of imagination are what set them apart from the crowd.

SCHEDULE AND LIFESTYLE

Video game designers that work for game studios and entertainment companies usually work 40 hours, five days a week. They may work longer when a deadline is approaching or when a problem comes up in the development process.

Freelance designers work a bit differently. For the most part, freelance designers can create their own schedules. A schedule is a plan of things to get done with times for accomplishing them. However, freelance designers must manage their time well in order to meet clients' deadlines.

As with any creative job, it can be helpful for designers to take breaks. This can refresh their imaginations and help them find new solutions.

Working long hours on a computer can be hard! Finding ways to stand and move during the day can help designers clear their minds.

SALARY AND PROSPECTS

A video game designer's salary, or yearly earnings, depends on their level of experience, education, and where they work. According to Glassdoor, a website for work-related conversations, the average salary for a video game designer in the United States is about $94,307. This field is growing quickly. Market researchers predict, or guess, that the game industry will grow by 8 percent from 2020 to 2027.

This is a fast-changing, fast-growing industry. **Virtual reality** gaming is being used more widely than ever. As gaming **technology** shifts and the demand for more games grows, designers have more opportunities, or chances, to make their mark in the field.

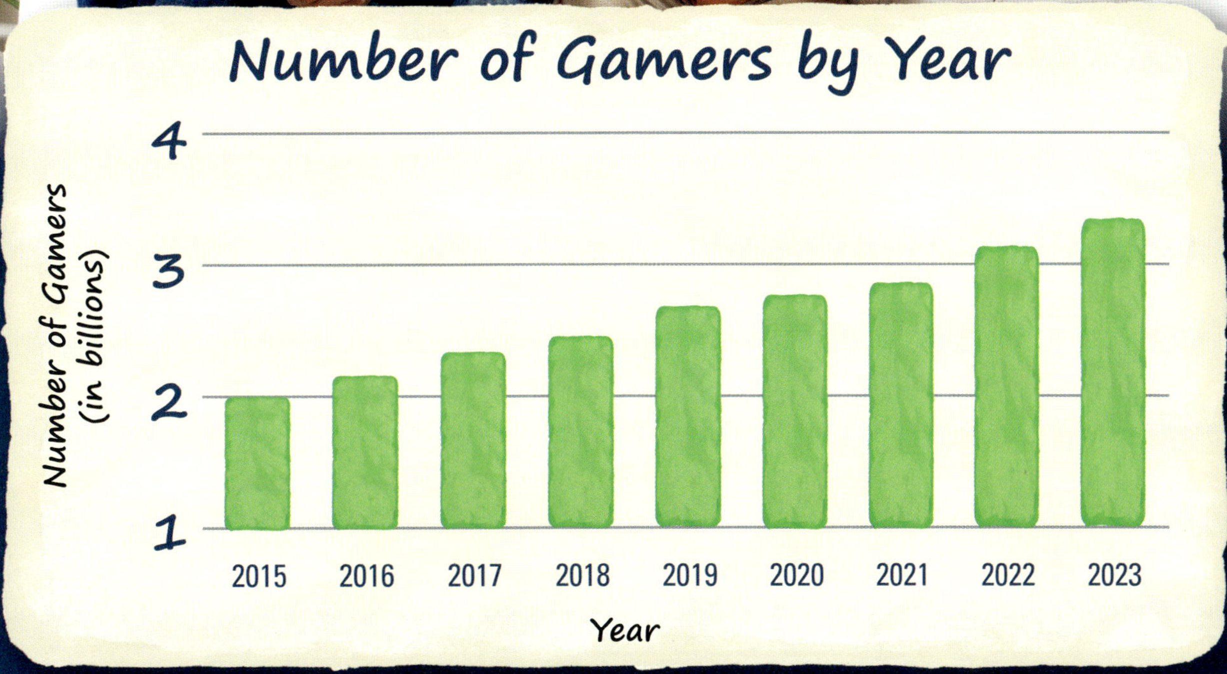

The number of gamers is growing by leaps and bounds. This means an increase in the field of video game design.

GET STARTED TODAY!

Does being a video game designer sound exciting to you? You don't have to wait until you're grown up to get started! Just play your favorite game and notice what you like about it. Pay attention to the storyline, the rules, and the mechanics. Think about what appeals to you or what you'd do differently.

Better yet, make up your own game! Write down your ideas and draw storyboards. Make an idea board with pictures of characters, settings, or colors you'd want to use. Ask your parent or caregiver to help you find a game design class online or other books about game design at your local library. Most importantly, develop your powers of imagination!

What video game worlds await inside your mind?

GLOSSARY

animate: Using computers to make art move in a lifelike way.

client: Someone who pays a professional for a certain service.

competitive: Having to do with something in which people try to beat others.

industry: A group of businesses that provide a certain product or service.

interactive: Involving the actions or inputs of a user.

professional: Having to do with a job someone does for a living.

studio: A building or room where an artist or artists work.

technical: Having special and usually practical knowledge, especially of a mechanical or scientific subject.

technology: Using science, engineering, and other industries to invent useful tools or to solve problems. Also a machine, piece of equipment, or method created by technology.

three-dimensional (3-D): Relating to something with three dimensions: height, width, and depth.

virtual: Artificial, or not real.

virtual reality: An artificial world made of images and sounds that's affected by the actions of the person who is experiencing it.

FOR MORE INFORMATION

BOOKS

Currie-McGhee, Leanne. *Hi-Tech Jobs in Video Gaming*. San Diego, CA: ReferencePoint Press, Inc., 2024.

Dougherty, Terri. *Jobs If You Like Video Games*. San Diego, CA: Reference Point Press, 2022.

WEBSITES

Inspire My Kids
inspiremykids.com/careers-that-count-so-you-want-to-be-a-video-game-designer/
Learn more about becoming a video game designer.

Science Buddies
www.sciencebuddies.org/science-fair-projects/project-ideas/video-computer-games
Try out a few video game design projects.

Publisher's note to educators and parents: Our editors have carefully reviewed these websites to ensure that they are suitable for students. Many websites change frequently, however, and we cannot guarantee that a site's future contents will continue to meet our high standards of quality and educational value. Be advised that students should be closely supervised whenever they access the internet.

INDEX